the Book of Ethel

By the same author:

Nervous Arcs (1995)
Botany Bay Document (1996)
The Hanging of Jean Lee (1998)
The Fall (2003)
Vertigo: A Cantata (2007)
the sonnet according to 'm' (2009)

the Book of Ethel

Jordie Albiston

PUNCHER & WATTMANN

© Jordie Albiston 2013

This book is copyright. Apart from any fair dealing for the purposes of study and research, criticism, review or as otherwise permitted under the Copyright Act, no part may be reproduced by any process without written permission. Inquiries should be made to the publisher.

First published in 2013
Published by Puncher and Wattmann
PO Box 441
Glebe NSW 2037

http://www.puncherandwattmann.com

puncherandwattmann@bigpond.com

National Library of Australia
Cataloguing-in-Publication entry:

Albiston, Jordie

the Book of Ethel

ISBN

I. Title.

A821.3

Cover design by Matthew Holt

Printed by McPhersons Printing Group

This project has been assisted by the Australian Government through the Australia Council, its arts funding and advisory body.

contents

so Life! we meet once more you	7
the Sun is sudden then hid	8
standing still! as a Standing-	9
Missus Cole from Cole's butcher-	10
Sunday after Wesley we	11
Tregeseal Nancharrow	12
bird *ydhyn* I watch Chough clip	13
pouting or pollack coley	14
to-day I sat on Guthrie's	15
measles diphtheria di-	16
Cornwall Home I take my leave	17
SS Iberia one	18
two days out from Plymouth third-	19
step off Iberia then	20
a pleasant run is made from	21
a piece of Anita a	22
a knock on Sydney Road door	23
Harold Overend handsome	24
you Collared but not by me	25
first church at last! a paddock	26
first parsonage 9 by 5	27
how I *hate* the *heat* in first	28
Mary Mary at my breast	29
we call her Isabel *she*	30
I did not know you Brother	31
daughter daughter daughter daught-	32
there is a group of us I'm	33
I wanted a doll's pram I	34
you so often away me	35
a Cornish woman old sold	36
tin copper where there are Mines	37

what a Glorious spot New	38
staying at what will be New	39
at New Home lives circuit-horse	40
as I said to Police-man	41
we have a small paddock halved	42
now I say if you borrow	43
strange so you haven't ever	44
I'm just Sick of sitting with	45
thank-you dear Mister in view	46
New Year's Eve 1930	47
the grand manor stands beneath	48
Mister says what here? a trove	49
Mont Albert Road Balwyn! so	50
we stayed there on Saturday	51
Mister writes Mother dear just	52
I recall my first pocket	53
you can tell I am unused	54
I've been to the wonderful	55
now you know they talk of this	56
I walked Balwyn to Belford	57
Mister takes Lizzie to Burke	58
we went out on that long jaunt	59
will you teach me how to make	60
dear me how many years since	61
Mister writes dear old Mother	62
Saturday VFL at	63
visualise the parsonage	64
you know if you cannot Sleep	65
dear Mister *how* have I missed	66
glossary	67

☙

so Life!   we meet once more   you
& I   in concert   concord
happy agreement to do
until done   my act   your stage
make   lie in it   this! my bit-
part   play   World   with me aboard
a Speck!   & then   *gigantic*

☙

the Sun is sudden   then hid
again   some-thing all about
the house   thro the glass   eyelids
twitch   Xmas in Penwith at
last!   & then many feet   ten!
or more!   up- & down-stairs   out
my door   *Quick!   Abandon bed!*

☙

standing still! as a Standing-
Stone I daren't breathe but be
found   Lucy gets bored but sing-
ing pretends calling *Where is
that hwerydh mine?*   she won't find
me   she doesn't try   Lucy-
Too-Old-For-Games   but Bernard

is *konnyk*   a Clever Boy
& I will hide till east meets
west   (how I like to annoy
him best!)   at last   Supper-bell
& Ethel! has won   she has
to slip in   give Thanks   & eat
(brother *hardened as Pharaoh!*)

☙

Missus Cole from Cole's butcher-
y likes to smile at the men
she says *Thank-you m'lover*
when one holds the door   he says
Orright m'bird   then   a word
I can't hear   it spoken
behind hands   joke!   *gesyow!*   Grand!

☙

Sunday   after Wesley   we
run the mile   wild garlic!   wood-
sage!   ragwort!   gorse!   thrift! down the
cliffs! to Penanwell   pilchards
crabs   herring & blennies   can?
I catch you   First! to be *good*
(of course I am Number Two)

ah Bernard   you brother you
better! than me   your net quite
filled for Stargazey Pie to-
night   Mother will love you &
Father be proud   sing aloud
Bernard has pyskador sight!
(I sit   bite tongue   swallow pride)

☙

Tregeseal   Nancharrow
I follow the stream   even
eels & stone-loach gone now
Father says   *arsnicky sluice!*
the fish all drowned   Mother sounds
from hot hob   *God bless! Bennen*
Mine   my feet sink thro slick slime

I see bal-maidens   racking
bucking   cobbing   sorting the
Deads up at grass   men hacking
rock   chucking black pastie-crusts
to the dark   (we Live   then we
Die   I follow the stream   see
it green   *make a wish*   dream fish)

☙

bird   *ydhyn*   I watch   Chough clip
across croft   bird   Kestrel stuck
there! aloft   Chaffinch it dips
& Yellow-hammer flits thro
green grass   Greenfinch on black winch
fair above bal   beneath muck-
heap   no bird   but Men   down there

☙

pouting or pollack　coley
or cod　whatever the catch
to-day　they trudge back slowly
to hearth & to Home　while we
lay dinner-plates　(women wait
for men with nets　women watch
for mackerel watch for men)

☙

to-day I sat on Guthrie's
bed   beneath the stunted oak
& played my toes in lovely
pink-bell heather   & wondered
whether *our poor little maw*
is well in Heaven   & spoke
a Prayer   for both of us   Home

❦

measles   diphtheria   di-
arrhoea   words I hear
thro the Night   *whooping-cough   vi-*
olence   cholera   Fate   words
I know well   then this one   *em-*
i-grate   new to the ear
the frightening   exciting   sound

em-i-grate   I am told it
means "to go"   but will there be
kerrek & croft   *karn* & quoit
where we "go"?   will New Home have
field & valley?   zawn?   wall?
will friends be waiting for me?
em-i-grate   emigrate   *so*

☙

Cornwall   Home   I take my leave
leave you alone   *all you brought
me*   set my mast   smile   grieve
Good-bye!   Good-bye!   Good-bye!   o
the boat   it waits   a World's gate
opens   finally   your daught-
er thro   Fare-well!   fair Home   thee

☙

SS Iberia   one
year older than me!   iron
hull   3 sail-masts   2 fun-
nels   single screw   & a speed
of 14 knots   linger not
good ship out-bound for Melbourne
Full Steam   a-hoy!   to New Home

☙

two days out from Plymouth   third-
class passenger Edward Sage
down with Delirium   slurs
Good-bye   & dies   the seas rise
& one month on   Fire-man John
Clark thrown to deck   *eight steerage
passengers strewn atop*   a

week of Peritonitis
he dies   our Captain Shannon
has us pray   chat   reminisce
the Usual Amusements
to kill off death   drown distress
we sing with spirit   each *on
song*   tho my own   stays below

☙

step off Iberia then
onto Italy   Light!   Col-
our!   Colour!   Light!   I see them
& buy them   the prettiest
Venetian beads   "light" recedes
but not so fast   beautiful!
roses   set in blue-glass   last

☙

a pleasant run is made from
Naples   where our Steamer called
we enter new Canal   on
time   & depart the Suez
28th ult   *men consult!*
contrary winds gust & squall!
till Cape Leuwin   rounded   *just*

a landing at Albany
spot-on 22nd inst
Australia!   finally!
we receive a few more guests
then! Adelaide   then! conveyed
thro rain & dread   a Clear Rinse!
then! Port Phillip Heads   then!   Here

☙

a piece of Anita   a
presence of Lucy   odds   sods
to *stitch them in mind*   far   far
where memory   strays   in Time
a Henderson hand-me-down
Trahair trousseau   somebody's
face-kerchief   lappet-cap   bow

my bodkin flies   feather-stitch
herring-bone   tying off Scraps
in a patch-work of   Find it!
Trace it!   Cut it!   to fit   then
puzzle the pieces   sew this
to   that   oblong   oval   trap-
ezoid   square   Place it!   here   there

☙

a knock on Sydney Road door
Mother   Loisa   me   Survey-
Lady says   *the Right is for*
All the People   not just Half
(I am only 19)   she
says   *Monster Petitions weigh*
heavy in Parliament   look

300 yards pure linen
30,000 signatures
Sign! with our suffrage Women
Victoria needs your Vote
it sparks the mind   each aligned
& we   all three   game   *Sign!*   sure
a name may some-how   make   mark

☙

Harold Overend   handsome
ordained   hands me a Package
on Xmas day   book   black   some-
thing has changed!   *to dear*   *with love*
my initials engraved   shall
we Open onto same Page?
walk   talk   coming-of-age   *both*

☙

you   Collared   but not by me
alone   your heart shared   above
below   on Earth as it be
in Heaven   *dear one*   don't choose!
Mister   Reverend   concur
you are two   revered   beloved
Husband-Husband   wedded   *Twice*

☙

first church at last!   a paddock
in Red Cliffs   10 miles from
Mildura   the landscape stock-
still   clear!   fell!   make way for God!
a cubby-size narthex   skies
resting on Heaven   my dom
my Methodist monk in the

yard   6 windows 2 gables
as Bleak! as can be   tree-stump-
fence-post   but we are able
the parish will come   over
time   this is the Call   & we
reply   our joy   never slump
or fall   Husband   & I   *Signed*

☙

first parsonage   9 by 5
white white   corrugated tin
card-table veranda   we've
no porthole to let Light in
but it does   & we fit!   hand-
some as family   lambkin
Heloisa   white white   in arms

& a fence   will be built   just
like St Just   o *this* is Land's
End! o new Cornwall!   I must
muster Home   the rest *over*
time   the new me   century
aligned   1900 stand-
ing   sentinel-straight   straight   white

☙

how I *hate* the *heat* in first
Home!   one cowers while cooking
in lean-to scullery   worse!
than Africa with skillion
roof   Mister laughs on behalf
of the sight   a Wife frying
sprats   while sporting Sunday hat!

☙

Mary   Mary   at my breast
in the centre of the night
all around they lull at rest
sisters three your Father the
sea   smell the salt!   feel the jolts
of God's good air give you might!
breathe safe in my arms tonight

Mary   Mary   one month young
so lively   & then so still
Sing! until your song is sung
& your reason to be   is
Done   we have chosen the coast
where Hovers the Hope   *God will*
fix Daddy's tickety-tock

Mary   Mary   contrary
quite!   what do you think of that?
suckling while dreamers ferry
their way   from darkness   back to
light   *sleep now*   Mary   *Brown Bear's*
here   let your Heart pitter-pat
all day all night   Stay   Keep   *dear*

☙

we call her Isabel   *she
has Isabel's eyes*   Mother
cries   Heloisa & Kally
delight   another tiny-
tot! in the House   our Cup does
augment   dear Mister *dears* her
(Mary   too young   for Comment)

☙

I did not know you Brother
John   (dead at 6)   nor Sister
Isabel   nor another
Brother (Guthrie)   (not yet 1)
(nor 1)   you did not Stay   bid
Fare-well as Fledglings   missed For-
ever by our Mother   tho

the Nest was full   but now I
miss you too   & wonder *who*
& *who* & *who*   & how my
own will stay Alive   Number
5 still safe inside   coming
soon   awaited waifs imbue
such Love   Wave!   then say *Adieu*

❧

daughter   daughter   daughter   daught-
er   son   & one inside   Home
at half-past 5   all I sought
has come to me   *as I was*
going to St Ives   re-paint!
the house!   I am not! alone
o   *what do you think I made*

out of my old herring's breast?
I sing   at night   after the
day   behold my fold   at Rest
remember the rest at old
St Just   & pray   for today
forever!   that none of thee
a-begging of barley   bread

❧

there is a group of us   I'm
not sure who we are   for all
I know we may be God's! prime
choir   you are   certain   centre
with me   as ever   *my Eve*
you say   & I say   *my All*
Stay!   Love!   until kingdom come

☙

I wanted a doll's pram   I
did not tell any-one   years
later my Father spoke   *why?*
did you not ask it it would
have been given   a sermon-
in-a-nutshell   some-thing clear
another God in the House!

do you see the fanciful
faces of our dolls in those
days?   blue eyes flaxen hair   real!
I shall not forget the shock
I got finding Dulcie in
the grasses by Mother's rose-
garden   forlorn & forgot

her look   soft   disfigured   a
melt   I stood horrified   Shot
& she so undone   all day
in the Sun   it seems to have
stopped up a part of my Heart
I remember a friend   not
one I know now   who promised

a doll   & when she had sent
& it came in the week the
feel of Grave Disappointment
for it was dressed as a boy!
a green-velvet suit!   I wept
again   I did not think they
made them men   I liked it   not

☙

you   so often away   me
so often a-waiting you
everyone wanting to see
their   Minister   *my*   Mister
tending your Flock   Tick-tock   Tock
horse & buggy dusty shoes
please stop   & knock   Home   *alone*

☙

a Cornish woman   old   sold
famous pepper-mint sweets she
composed herself   emboldened
by my greed   I would enter
stand straight & plea the lady
in the towser   *a penny-*
worth of stomach-warmers please

still in my nights I linger
within   that threshold   past   the
outside beckons   & I spin
stare-up against windows tight
with many knots of glass   plot
to see thro but cannot   they
let in Light   but not *the view*

☙

tin   copper   where there are Mines
there you will find the Cornish-
man   I remember a Mine-
Captain's girl   the fine boots she
wore   back from America
running *right up the leg*   with
curious laces   circus-

top tassles   *style* the yard-
stick here   while mine alas! all
strength & caps   just like Bernard's
how it tickled!   old Mister
Rhodda sizing my foot   sing-
ing *width! height! length!* as he scrawled
see   I was a "climber"   then

☙

what a Glorious spot   New
Hobart Home   *why the mountain!*
in our back-yard!   morning view
trees creep up slowly thro rays
Borealis Australis
pink fingers at mid-night   stain
Organ Pipes   summit   in Light

Mister   mighty!   *loud* then *low*
fills convict-built Wesley church
we have a Square   four narrow
pews   cedar   front-right   with a
Gate to go thro   we sit so
Up-lifted   our private perch
I like it not   from such height

☙

staying at what will be New
Home   the Husbands *arranging
things*   dear Mister concedes to
Type-writer   but Queenie the
Cow   No Fear!   *he* can't milk   *he*
won't learn   That's That   I just sing
Meanie   (Mister doesn't Hear)

☙

at New Home lives circuit-horse
Dick   & Queenie (!)   who kindly
provides us with milk   (of course
butter is scarce when a house-
hold of 10 *craves* more than *saves*
enough cream)   while dear Queenie
muses on cud   our youngest

two Margaret & Best climb
her ribs   slide! down the other
side   8 pounds she cost a Fine
Buy   the only Frost   her calves
always Boys   a match when Fat
Hen hatches 12 brat-roosters
while inside Girls! rule the Pen

ʚ

as I said to Police-man
Harmon   I stepped out from Home
8 minutes to 11
returning 20 past 12
rings brooches purses   dispersed
& some 30 pounds-worth   Gone!
Venetian beads!   thro breakfast-

room window   open   its wire
torn awry   well they caught him
in New Town   charged him with Liar
Arthur James Walton   my best!
in a bundle!   I'm told he'll
sport guiltlessness   Hobart crime
court   then   & beyond that   *God*

☙

we have a small paddock   halved
by a white wood fence   a board
well-greased   leant against   sends laugh-
ing children   *right out to grass!*
of course Mother! must try   her
grip slips   feet shot! Heaven-wards
bundled in barrow   wheeled Home

☙

now I say   if you borrow
a lovely   big   black   sitting-
hen from *that nice young fellow*
you'll lose your daughter   & we
did   without fuss he lends us
the hen   & as is fitting
(*15 chicks later!*)   hen is

returned   then   chickens eat wheat
for Xmas   but Old Rat knocks
breaks thro   his own Festive treat!
just one tiny-tot survives
grows fat! & brown   now allowed
to scratch in yard   Mister's fox-
terrier cannot resist

tackled once more   she survives
once more   I offer whole maize
Special Fancy   alas! five
days on   Brave   she dies   put to
rest   rose-garden   *lose a hen*
lose a daughter   but give Praise
a crop!   from Missus Brown's grave

☙

strange   so you haven't ever
a Purse   but to such Souls what
is money?   slow   the silver
is counted   & from its pile
a sixpence   taken   a zack-
in-hand for the tiny-tot
kind Hearts *more* than Coronets

೦ಜ

I'm just Sick of sitting with
my eye peering thro a hole
in the lattice   lean-to   *breathe*
to hear hobnailed heels   jolly
rattle of latch   merry snatch
of Hullo-a cheer my soul
life is so dull without you

I simply wait & sit wait-
ing   he   Mister   gone off to
camp in the hills   o too late
for me   *dear what's a canoe?*
his word that it only fits
One   my word   if I could go
that World would some-how hold Two

here sit I in the back-yard
alone but for Missus Black-
Orpington   who wants regard
yet isn't allowed   if I
venture near she doubles the
size   & flies at me   *come back*
I shout! to my Scout   *back Home*

☙

thank-you dear Mister   in view
of the present sent   Mission
Cookery Book   *the Value*
of Cooked Bones   yes!   a varied
& pounce-upon Collection
(I sit reading   yet wishing
you   & your *presence*   at Home)

☙

New Year's Eve   1930
all well   tho the Gripes in Marg-
aret's hands have forced early
Fare-well to Piano   a
shame   such skill to have it go
while so young   yet   her smile *large*
complains not   Siz & Kally

& Mary in health   our chap
Best   (21 soon!)   sound on
Life's path   & Loisa   happy
too   Mister fluctuates   *God
heal his good Heart*   but apart
from this ill never flounders
as for me   I am thankful

what Abundance!   a rail to
rest this old leg on   a leg
to rest on this rail   too few
hours perhaps   per day   but
a whole New Year shines bright   clear
I   neither frail   nor fraught   beg
nothing   lack lesser   than Nought

☙

the grand manor stands beneath
what we eat   blue windows blue
trees & that Masonware sheath
of white! sky   patent iron-
stone china   from Home   we throng
& sweet grace ladles into
each mouth   tastes   the Master's plate

☙

Mister says   what here?   a trove
a life   a well-woven peek
my writerly Wife   who loves
to Tell   a Tome of your own
sly outing   a sum   era
on paper   *"Parsonage Peeps"*
card-cover saddle-stapled

etchings & drawings   & all
for a mere 1&6   I
am so proud to see your Scrawl
type-set   trained   now to be Sold
Ethel Overend   ever
a name   imagine that   my
own blue-stockinged Heroine

☙

Mont Albert Road   Balwyn!   so
many churches   so many
Homes   Red Cliffs   Mildura   to
Warracknabeal   then Queenscliff
Prahran   & then over the
Strait to Launceston! when we
stop for 3 years   then New Town

(4 years)   then Hobart (for 5)
back over the water   (4
fleghes still in tow)   we arrive
in Kew (another 5 years)
then Malvern South (fewer mouths
to feed)   2 years at Hawthorn
then Here   (pull-up)   (un-pack)   (*breathe*)

☙

we stayed there on Saturday
night   & I said to Mister
*I don't like low-lying place-
s*   but this was delightful
cool as the Dandenongs   &
you know how refreshed we were
when we woke   with the Light!   up

☙

Mister writes   Mother dear   just
a line   or two   to say how
well I love & miss you   Best
& Mary & beloveds
at Alec T's house to tea
Best here all yesterday   now
Mary & Best to tea   The

Bishop to tea at Alec
E's   there & back per car Miss
Helen as chauffeuse   soon Dick
for tea   Polly's for supper
come Home   Do   & save this man
with your constant hand from his
speeding to certain Ruin

☙

I recall my first pocket
do you?   wasn't it thrilling
to *slip in* hand & lock on
a currant in the corner
but pockets & currants stand
off from fashion these fun-filled
days   (pack towser back   in robe)

☙

you can tell I am unused
to talking   there was a plan
for Tasmania   I chose
to help my Mister at all
the meetings &   understand
I slept 12! beds in that land
each day another forum

each night another bed   more!
hundreds! of people to meet
& greet   a gentle-man swore
you know   you give greater than
the Reverend Overend
15 or 20 words each
minute   now that is! a thing

well   Friends   if you buy a small
car you may gain 40 miles
to the gallon after-all
yet if you get a Hudson
super-six you will accrue
but 18 miles   now which style
would you choose to travel in?

☙

I've been to the wonderful
city-to-be! & learning
geography under the
go-there system I find my-
self 2,000 feet high &
there *Canberra* I can bring
no picture of what it was

like because there is no-where
in Victoria that I
can tell you Look & compare
but Friends it is a delight!
with valleys & hill-views &
a comfortable climate why
who needs another hot rush!

long long years ago when
I first knew Mister Bowring
he & the boys (how I en-
vied them) took a trip out to
Canberra none yet had gone
"Duntroon! Duntroon!" excepting
the Lads but now then I have

☙

now you know they talk of this
piece-in-the-middle as the
territory   like some is-
land   apart   kept from the rest
&   heat aside   call it dry
yet Queanbeyan exports there
thousands   *thousands!*   of jug-loads

of beer each month   I ask   *who*
drinks them?   but don't like to Judge
road-makers line-workers queued
beneath Sun   parched   arch-backed   &
houses like miner-camps   I
cannot tell   if with such drudge
one could be   tee-total   then

☙

I walked Balwyn to Belford
Road   to give little Lizzie
Biggest Lolly in the World!
she watched me search Purse   eyes large
as tea-saucers   until her
hand clasped it   the most tiny
cure-em-quick   o!   kick Granny!

☙

Mister takes Lizzie to Burke
Road shops   Mac   fox-terrier
always at Heel   the store-clerk
smiles   *a sixpence for block-pad*
to colour in   a florin
for packet of pencils   her
little hands are full   hand in

hand   grand-father   grand-daughter
crumb-cake & tea   peaceful in
Camberwell   no WWII
here   I fear for dear Cousins
sweet Cornwall   & Bombs   then stand
Stop   when I hear them come in
Granny!   we've been to the shops!

☙

we went out on that long jaunt
the jaunt that made me Famous
because I scribbled   & sent
on spec to the Spectator
& they put! it in   a bit
about Canberra   just us
in the back of a motor-

bus   with twin wicker chairs side-
by-side   it was so hot &
we were so tight that   as I
had wrote   our poor Mister felt
like an *antiphlogistine*
plaster beside me   I had
to go   sit away   a-while

☙

*will you teach me how to make
Cornish pasties?* she asks   tho
I'm happy   with cheery crack-
ling fire   giant mountain
bearing forests on its crest
saw-milling sounds zinging thro
the air   & my Vow not to

cook for an entire sennight
I comply   chop mother-of-
pearl onion   ivory-white
potato   butter-colour
swede   roll pastry   speak freely
all the while kneading sweet love
for thee   *sweet* Cornwall   sweet Home

a fishing fleet sailing thro
west-slanting Sun   layer on
layer   a twist then a skew
& sit by the oven   as
memories rise   open eyes
lay cloth call men   *hurry!   Home!*
tiddy-oggy   golden   Done

☙

dear me   how many years since
I first sat in Sunday school
a Life!   yet I am convinced
it is *yesterday*   I must
have been wee   hence I was sent
first with Bernard   I recall
his hand-kerchief rolled to a

ball   him wiping my nose   right
over my face!   (later it
felt uncomfortable   quite)
the Bibles were brought tied with
cord   if the boys made a noise
they were hit! with the cord   but
not too hard I think   now   I

remember one Sunday our
form falling backwards   a row
of *sweet girls*   feet in the air
my white lace socks my two black
shoes with a button sewed at
each toe in the air!   o!   how
I miss those days   being there

☙

Mister writes   dear old Mother
just a few lines to greet you
Sweet-heart & Wife for over
45 years   this your
birthday morning   & praying
a day free! from the Pains you
have bravely endured   new news

of the good night's rest & sleep
you have explained was the best
news I have heard   may you keep
in full swing for many a
climb   you know   my old Heart lies
in yours   yours in mine   God bless
you   more Splendid   over time

☙

Saturday   VFL at
Windy Hill or MCG
this is not *hurling!*   I bat
my flag   dole out displeasure
BAD DECISION!   grand-children
redden   *mortified*   Granny!
(Sunday   good Methodist Wife)

☙

visualise the parsonage
beds you have slept in   count all
the cribs that have been yours   gauge
them Good tho one shall not! be
forgot   Admit!   Bad!   call it
Hammock Brand   Beware! night-fall
caught in a Slack Wire Affair

perhaps no Minister had
thought   *screw up these ends*   any-
how that's how dear Mister &
I got heaped! together one
year   now   I have the most love-
ly cradle   Good Nights many
but alas you   Gone   to Sleep

☙

you know   if you cannot Sleep
folk say   count sheep   coming thro
gaps in the hedge   well   my sheep
jump hedge   turn back   run away
with such a rush   they get Stuck
then scamper off   no time to
count any-thing!   but   *Tick*   *Tock*

☙

dear Mister   *how* have I missed
you   That Instant   open gate
Gone   my Heart   empty   amiss
without you   one year on   too
long!   enough Life   for this Wife
what's a door?   but a way straight
thro   & I am going   too

glossary

bal	mine, especially tin
fleghes	children
gesyow	joke
hwerydh	sister
karn	cairn, tor
kerrek	rock
konnyk	clever
maw	boy
pyskador	fisherman
quoit	neolithic structure, with standing stones supporting capstone
sennight	one week
tiddy-oggy	pastie
towser	apron
ydhyn	bird
zack	sixpence
zawn	chasm, cut by erosion into sea cliff

acknowledgements

These poems are about my maternal great grandmother, Ethel Overend, née Trahair. Ethel was born in 1872 (St Just, Cornwall) and died in 1949 (Melbourne). She married the Reverend Harold Overend in 1898, and together they raised six children: Heloisa, Kathleen (Kally), Mary, Isabel (Siz), Best and Margaret (Marsi). Marsi gave birth to one child, Elisabeth, my mother.

☙

Great appreciation is extended to the Australia Council for the Arts for funding a four-week residency at the Jamieson Library in Newmill, Cornwall, during September 2011: archival materials are a necessary element to any documentary poetry, but nothing compares to the witness of place.

My gratitude to Melissa Hardie of the Hypatia Trust (Cornwall) for providing warm support and a quiet place to live and work during my residency.

Recognition is due to Mark Taylor, who accessed an indispensable array of genealogical facts and related historical information. Others who contributed to my concept of Ethel — by offering objects, photographs, memories, anecdotes — include Elisabeth Albiston, Max Albiston, Philippa James, Jane Green and Douglas Atkins.

To readers Elisabeth Albiston, Max Albiston, Andrea Goldsmith, John Leonard, Wendy Morris and Andy Szikla, your help took various forms: it created a stronger work. Thank you.

www.ingramcontent.com/pod-product-compliance
Lightning Source LLC
Chambersburg PA
CBHW030813090426
42737CB00010B/1257